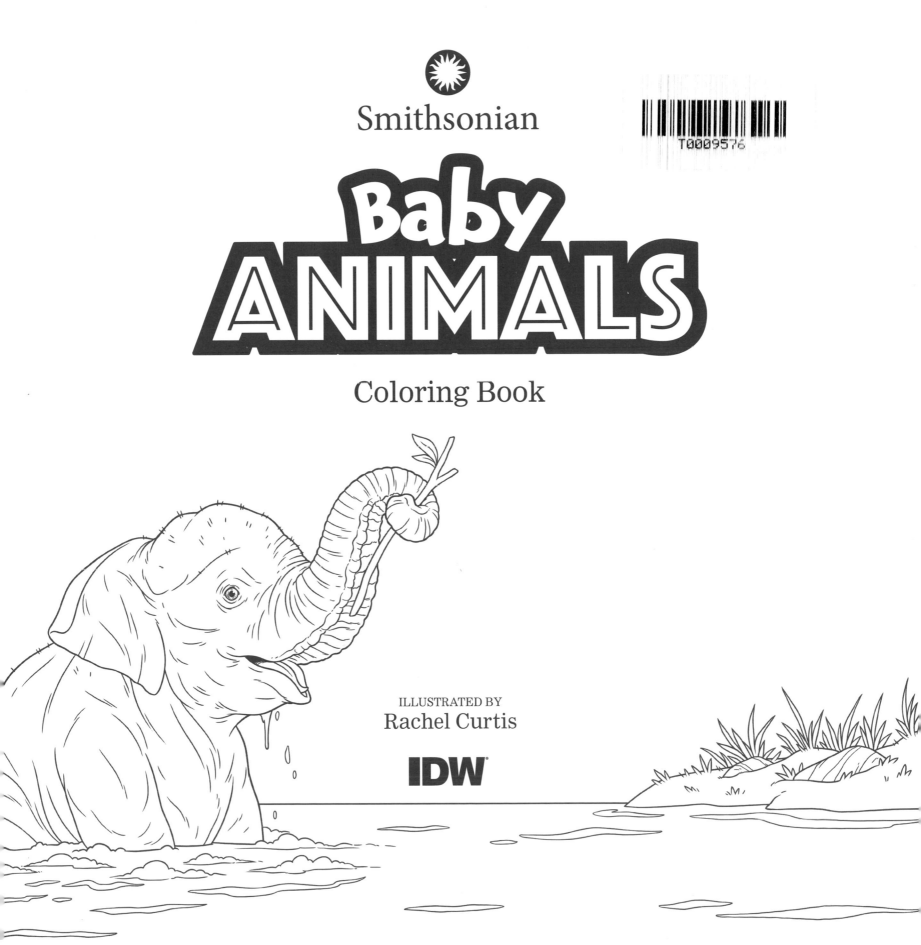

Smithsonian

Baby ANIMALS

Coloring Book

ILLUSTRATED BY
Rachel Curtis

IDW

@idwpublishing
idwpublishing.com

ISBN : 978-1-68405-954-6   26 25 24 23   1 2 3 4

TEXT BY
SMITHSONIAN'S NATIONAL ZOO AND CONSERVATION BIOLOGY INSTITUTE

ILLUSTRATIONS BY
RACHEL CURTIS

EDITED BY
ALONZO SIMON

EDITORIAL ASSISTANCE BY
ZAC BOONE

BOOK DESIGN BY
NATHAN WIDICK

Nachie Marsham, Publisher
Blake Kobashigawa, SVP Sales, Marketing & Strategy
Mark Doyle, VP Editorial & Creative Strategy
Tara McCrillis, VP Publishing Operations
Anna Morrow, VP Marketing & Publicity
Alex Hargett, VP Sales
Jamie S. Rich, Executive Editorial Director
Scott Dunbier, Director, Special Projects
Greg Gustin, Sr. Director, Content Strategy
Kevin Schwoer, Sr. Director of Talent Relations
Lauren LePera, Sr. Managing Editor

Keith Davidsen, Director, Marketing & PR
Topher Alford, Sr. Digital Marketing Manager
Patrick O'Connell, Sr. Manager, Direct Market Sales
Shauna Monteforte, Sr. Director of Manufacturing Operations
Greg Foreman, Director DTC Sales & Operations
Nathan Widick, Director of Design
Neil Uyetake, Sr. Art Director, Design & Production
Shawn Lee, Art Director, Design & Production
Jack Rivera, Art Director, Marketing

Ted Adams and Robbie Robbins, IDW Founders

Special thanks to the team at the Smithsonian for all of their assistance and support.

Smithsonian Enterprises:
Kealy Gordon, Product Development Manager
Jill Corcoran, Director, Licensed Publishing
Brigid Ferraro, VP, Consumer and Education Products
Carol LeBlanc, President

Smithsonian's National Zoo and Conservation Biology Institute:

Tony Barthel, Curator
Leighann Cline, Animal Keeper
Hilary Colton, Animal Keeper
Christ Crowe, Animal Keeper
Sara Hasenstab, Animal Keeper
Matt Evans, Assistant Curator

Sara Hallager, Curator, Bird House
Kenton Kerns, Assistant Curator
Becky Malinsky, Curator
Alan Peters, Curator
Dolores Reed, Supervisory Biologist
Erica Royer, Animal Keeper

Craig Saffoe, Curator
Rebecca Sturniolo, Assistant Curator
Laurie Thompson, Assistant Curator
Jen Zoon, Communications Specialist

The Smithsonian's National Zoo and Conservation Biology Institute is one of Washington D.C.'s most popular tourist destinations. The Zoo instills a lifelong commitment to conservation through engaging experiences with animals and the people working to save them. Founded in 1889, the Zoo is part of the Smithsonian Institution, the world's largest museum and research complex. Today, it is home to 2,700 animals representing more than 390 species. The Zoo leads the Smithsonian's global effort to save species, better understand ecosystems and train future generations of conservationists.

The publisher would like to thank The Cornell Lab of Ornithology's All About Birds and The National Wildlife Federation for providing additional information.

GIANT PANDA

Ailuropoda melanoleuca

Where are they from?

Giant pandas are native to south central China, in the Sichuan, Shaanxi, and Gansu provinces. They once lived in lowland areas, but farming, forest clearing, and other development now restrict giant pandas to the mountains. The International Union for Conservation of Nature lists the giant panda as vulnerable to extinction.

Fun Fact #1: Panda pregnancies last between 90 and 180 days, with an average pregnancy lasting 135 days. This wide variation in gestation occurs because the fertilized egg usually floats freely in the mother's uterus before it implants and begins developing.

Fun Fact #2: Giant panda cubs are born pink, hairless, and blind. They weigh 3 to 5 ounces (85 to 142 grams) and are about the size of a stick of butter at birth. At 1/900th the size of its mother, a giant panda cub is the smallest mammal newborn relative to its mother's size, except for a marsupial, such as a kangaroo or opossum.

Fun Fact #3: At around one year old, a panda cub's diet is mostly made up of bamboo and other solid foods. But cubs may nurse for comfort up to 18 months of age.

KOMODO DRAGON

Varanus komodoensis

Where are they from?

Komodo dragons are limited to a few Indonesian islands of the Lesser Sunda group, including Rintja, Padar, and Flores, and, of course, the island of Komodo, which is the largest at 22 miles (35 kilometers) long. Komodo dragons live in tropical savanna forests but range widely over the islands, from beach to ridge top.

Fun Fact #1: Females lay about 30 eggs in depressions dug on hill slopes or within the pilfered nests of megapodes—large, chicken-like birds that make nests of heaped earth mixed with twigs that may be as long as 3 feet (1 meter) in height and 10 feet (3 meters) across.

Fun Fact #2: While the eggs incubate in the nest for about nine months, the female may lay on the nest to protect the eggs. No evidence of parental care for newly hatched Komodo dragons exists.

Fun Fact #3: The hatchlings weigh less than 3.5 ounces (100 grams) and average 16 inches (40 centimeters) in length. Their early years are precarious, and they often fall victim to predators, including other Komodo dragons.

KORI BUSTARD

Ardeotis kori

Where are they from?

Kori bustards are large, terrestrial birds native to the eastern and southern regions of Africa. They inhabit wide, open grasslands and lightly wooded savanna. Their numbers have rapidly declined in the wild due to habitat destruction, hunting, and slow reproduction rate.

Fun Fact #1: In the wild, a male kori reaches sexual maturity around five years of age. At that time, he will display—toss his head, gulp air, and make booming calls—to impress potential mates.

Fun Fact #2: As with all bustards, the clutch of one to two eggs is laid on the ground in a shallow scrape the female has made.

Fun Fact #3: The eggs are pale olive in color, with splotches of brown. Incubation lasts 23 to 24 days. The chicks hatch fully developed and remain with the female well after the fledging period, the time it takes to develop the feathers needed to fly, which in this case is about five weeks.

SUMATRAN TIGER

Panthera tigris ssp. sumatrae

Where are they from?

Tigers are found in a variety of habitats across South and Southeast Asia, China, and Eastern Russia. They thrive in temperate, tropical, or evergreen forests, mangrove swamps, and grasslands. Sumatran tigers are found only on the Indonesian island of Sumatra. Globally, tigers are considered an endangered species. The Sumatran subspecies is considered critically endangered by the International Union for Conservation of Nature. It is estimated that between 400 and 500 exist in the wild.

Fun Fact #1: Gestation lasts approximately 100 days, and females give birth to between two and four cubs.

Fun Fact #2: Once cubs become independent, at about age two, females are ready to give birth again.

Fun Fact #3: Like other big cats, tigers can't purr, but they sure can roar. Tigers also bellow, grunt, and chuff, and they use scent marking as another form of communication.

SCREAMING HAIRY ARMADILLO

Chaetophractus vellerosus

Where are they from?

Found just east of the Andes Mountains, in the Monte Desert, screaming hairy armadillos inhabit parts of Argentina, Bolivia, and Paraguay. They prefer a dry habitat with loose, sandy soil, which allows for easier burrowing—an important part of this animal's survival. These armadillos have been observed living in open areas such as sand dunes, savannas, pastures, and agricultural areas at altitudes up to 3,280 feet (1,000 meters).

Fun Fact #1: This species typically breeds in the fall months and gives birth after a gestation period of 60 to 75 days.

Fun Fact #2: In the wild, female screaming armadillos are reproductively active in the winter and spring. The average litter size is two and screaming armadillos can have two or more litters a year. Newborn armadillos weigh just over 5 ounces (155 grams).

Fun Fact #3: Their eyes remain shut for about 16 to 30 days, and they wean from their mother when they are about two months old.

CUBAN CROCODILE

Crocodylus rhombifer

Where are they from?

Cuban crocodiles have the smallest range of any crocodile, encompassing an area less than 200 square miles (500 square kilometers). They are found only in Cuba's Zapata Swamp in the southwest and Lanier Swamp on Isla de Juventud. Their historical range also included the Cayman and Bahaman islands.

Cuban crocodiles prefer freshwater marshes and swamps similar to those of the Everglades. They rarely swim in saltwater. The Cuban crocodile is one of the most threatened New World crocodilian species, primarily because it has such a small and restricted distribution. Their main threat is humans, who have hunted the crocodile extensively and have largely encroached upon their habitats.

Fun Fact #1: Cuban crocodiles construct mound nests and lay an average of 30 to 40 eggs, though the number of eggs depends upon the size and age of the mother.

Fun Fact #2: The eggs range widely in size but, on average, are 2.5 inches (6 centimeters) long. In the wild, the eggs hatch about two and a half months after they are laid.

Fun Fact #3: The temperature of the nest determines the sex of the hatchlings. Between 89.6 and 90.5 degrees Fahrenheit (32 to 32.5 Celsius) produces males.

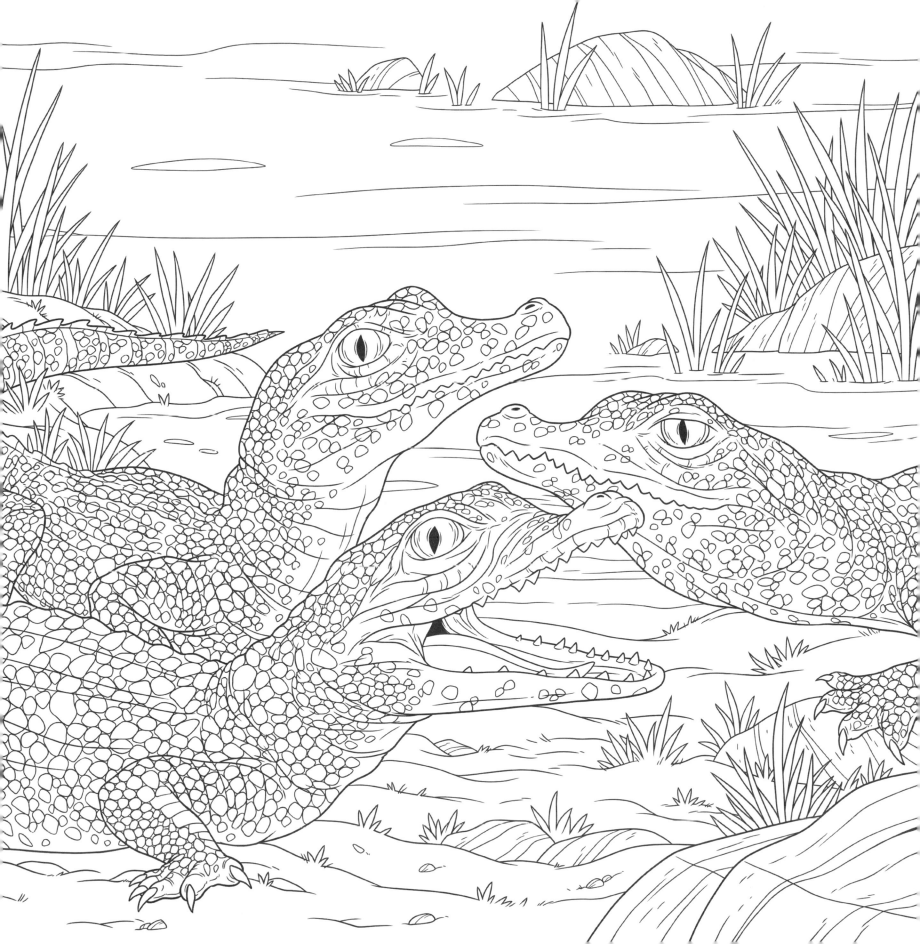

ORANGUTAN

Pongo abelii, Pongo pygmaeus, Pongo tapanuliensis

Where are they from?

Orangutans live on the Indonesian island of Sumatra and in both the Malaysian and Indonesian portions of the island of Borneo. They are highly arboreal and live in all levels of the forest, from floor to canopy. Habitats range from peat swamp forests near sea level to mountainous forests almost one mile (1.6 kilometers) above sea level. As humans have moved into the lower elevations—the orangutan's original habitat—orangutans have moved up the mountainsides. Bornean, Sumatran, and Tapanuli orangutans are critically endangered, primarily due to habitat loss.

Fun Fact #1: Orangutans usually have a single baby, and twins are rare. Gestation is about eight and a half months. From birth, orangutan infants cling to their mothers as they maneuver through the trees. The orangutan has the longest period of dependence on the mother of any land-dwelling animal, including humans.

Fun Fact #2: Infant orangutans can nurse until they are six to seven years old, though weaning is highly variable, depending on the mother. It is thought that weaning occurs sooner if food is abundant, so the infant can switch to solids.

Fun Fact #3: A female orangutan will only have a baby about every seven to nine years, resulting in only four or five babies in her lifetime. The inter-birth interval is somewhat longer in Sumatran orangutans than it is in Bornean orangutans. Researchers are still trying to determine why this is the case.

ASIAN ELEPHANT

Elephas maximus

Where are they from?

Asian elephants are found in isolated pockets of India and Southeast Asia. They were formerly widely distributed south of the Himalayas, throughout Southeast Asia, and in China as far north as the Yangtze River. Asian elephants are endangered.

Fun Fact #1: Gestation is between 21.5 and 22 months, the longest gestation period for any animal. Usually one calf (occasionally two) is born and weighs between 150 and 350 pounds (68 to 158 kilograms).

Fun Fact #2: Calves stand and nurse soon after birth. By six months, calves begin feeding on vegetation. For several years, they also eat their mother's dung and that of the other elephants in their herd, which contains nutrients as well as the symbiotic bacteria that aid in the digestion of cellulose.

Fun Fact #3: Weaning is a gradual process that may continue until the mother delivers another calf.

ALDABRA TORTOISE

Geochelone gigantea

Where are they from?

They are found on Aldabra Island, one of the Seychelles islands northeast of Madagascar in the Indian Ocean. Aldabra Island is a coral atoll bordered by jagged limestone and small beaches and encloses a large mangrove-bordered lagoon. The tortoises live in habitats such as scrub, mangrove swamp, and coastal dunes. The largest concentration of tortoises is found in the grasslands called platins.

Fun Fact #1: Females carry the eggs for about ten weeks, after which period they are buried in the ground. Clutch size is 9 to 25 tennis ball–sized eggs.

Fun Fact #2: Typically, only three to five viable young are produced from a clutch. In high-density populations, female Aldabras may only lay four to five eggs every few years, whereas in low-density populations, they may lay several clutches a year.

Fun Fact #3: Incubation is about four months.

RED PANDA

Ailurus fulgens

Where are they from?

Red pandas live in temperate, high-altitude forests with bamboo understories in the Himalayas and other high mountains. They range from northern Myanmar (Burma) to the southern Sichuan and Yunnan provinces of China. They are also found in suitable habitat in Nepal, India, and Tibet. *Ailurus fulgens fulgens* lives predominantly in Nepal and can also be found in India and Bhutan. *Ailurus fulgens styani* (or *Ailurus fulgens refulgens*) is primarily found in China and Myanmar. Red pandas are endangered and are legally protected in India, Bhutan, China, Nepal, and Myanmar. Their primary threats are habitat loss and degradation, human interference, and poaching.

Fun Fact #1: Females create a nest in tree holes, hollow stumps, tree roots, or bamboo thickets and line the nest with moss, leaves, and other soft plant material. Litters typically consist of two cubs born between May and July in the Northern Hemisphere.

Fun Fact #2: Red pandas are born completely covered in fur to protect them from the cold environment. Newborns of the species *Ailurus fulgens fulgens* weigh 3 to 4 ounces (about 90 to 110 grams).

Fun Fact #3: The offspring stay with the mother for about one year, which is about when they are full grown.

SCIMITAR-HORNED ORYX

Oryx dammah

Where are they from?

A century ago, hundreds of thousands of desert-adapted antelopes roamed the Sahara and Sahel regions of Northern Africa, a vast desert and sub-desert ecosystem that includes parts of Morocco, Tunisia, Algeria, Libya, Egypt, Mauritania, Mali, Niger, Chad, and Sudan.

Though once distributed across most of North Africa, scimitar-horned oryx are currently considered extinct in the wild due to a combination of widespread over-hunting, habitat loss, and persistent drought. A reintroduction project led by the Environment Agency—Abu Dhabi, which also includes the Sahara Conservation Fund, the Zoological Society of London, and the Smithsonian's National Zoo and Conservation Biology Institute, is working collaboratively with the government of Chad and the international zoo community to return oryx to their native habitat. The first release, consisting of 23 individuals bred in human care, began in 2016. Smithsonian scientists monitor the release of every animal via satellite tracking collars. The tracking collars provide data on oryx movements and survival, as well as a means for tracking and monitoring individuals on the ground through radio telemetry.

Fun Fact #1: About eight to eight and a half months after mating, females give birth to a single calf weighing about 22 pounds (10 kilograms).

Fun Fact #2: In 2021, SCBI scientists used CO-Synch—a protocol developed for the artificial insemination of livestock—to increase the chances that two female scimitar-horned oryx would successfully conceive. Reproductive physiologists used frozen-thawed semen that was originally collected from two different males 20 and 13 years ago. This scientific breakthrough enabled conservationists to bolster the genetic diversity of scimitar-horned oryx—both in human care and in their native Chad—while minimizing the need to physically transport animals between breeding facilities.

HENKEL'S LEAF-TAILED GECKO

Uroplatus henkeli

Where are they from?

As with all leaf-tailed geckos, they are endemic to the islands of Madagascar, which is known for being a biodiversity hotspot—80 to 90 percent of its animal and plant species are exclusive to the area. The biggest threat has been the continuous deforestation happening throughout Madagascar, which is aggravated by climate change.

Fun Fact #1: When they first hatch, Henkel's leaf-tailed geckos have some built-in energy reserves from their yolk sac. In the first 24 to 48 hours, they shed off their newborn skin—and that becomes their first meal.

Fun Fact #2: At the time of their hatching, Henkel's leaf-tailed geckos measure 2 to 3 inches (5 to 7.5 centimeters) in length (including the tail) and weigh about .07 ounces (2 grams). To put that in perspective: Adults can grow up to 11 inches (28 centimeters) in length; adult females weigh about 2.5 ounces (70 grams).

Fun Fact #3: These geckos are nocturnal and hunt mostly at night. Their specialized eyes give them incredible night vision, which helps them find small invertebrates in the trees. There is evidence that nocturnal geckos can see up to 350 times better than humans in dim light and may even see color at night!

BENNETT'S WALLABY

Macropus rufogriseus

Where are they from?

Bennett's wallabies are native to the eastern coast of Australia, from mid-Queensland south to Victoria and parts of South Australia. A significant population also exists in Tasmania. They are commonly found in eucalyptus forests and open areas with nearby tree shelter but can tolerate a diversity of habitats, including farmland.

Fun Fact #1: Breeding patterns for this species differ depending upon range. Populations in Tasmania tend to reproduce between January and July, with joeys born in greatest frequency in February and March. Mainland wallabies breed year-round, with most joeys born during the Southern Hemisphere's summer months: December, January, and February.

Fun Fact #2: After a gestation of just 29 days, Bennett's wallabies are born looking embryonic and weighing less than .04 ounces (1 gram). The newborn joeys are hairless and underdeveloped but have strong enough forelimbs to climb into their mothers' pouch. The single newborn then latches onto its mother's teat, where it continues to develop.

Fun Fact #3: Pouch life lasts for about nine months, but joeys remain with their mothers, continuing to nurse, for an additional three to nine months.

JAPANESE GIANT SALAMANDER

Andrias japonicus

Where are they from?

Japanese giant salamanders are native to Japan and can be found in the country's central highland mountainous regions. A few populations have also been discovered living on some of the smaller southern islands adjacent to the main island of Japan. Giant salamanders are mostly aquatic and live in cold, fast-flowing water, where oxygen is in good supply. These sites are often rivers in forested and mountainous areas. During the day, Japanese giant salamanders hide under large rocks along the water's edge to stay concealed.

Fun Fact #1: These salamanders spawn from August through October. During this season, they migrate upriver looking for "dens"—caverns or burrows, each containing a single underwater entrance. The largest, most dominant male in a territory of river will occupy the den and defend it.

Fun Fact #2: Females typically lay a clutch of 400 to 600 eggs. Once the females have laid their eggs and the male has fertilized them, the females leave the den. It is now the male's job to provide protection while the eggs develop and hatch.

Fun Fact #3: This incubation period ranges from 40 to 60 days. The male, sometimes referred to as the "den master," guards and protects the nest for a couple of months, until the juvenile salamanders go off on their own.

GUAM KINGFISHER (SIHEK)

Todiramphus cinnamominus

Where are they from?

This species was found only on the island of Guam but is extinct there today. All existing Guam kingfishers, or sihek (SEE-heck), as they are called in CHamoru (the language of the indigenous people of the Mariana Islands), are descended from 29 individuals. They were taken from the wild into human care in the 1980s to create a breeding program to save the species from extinction.

Historically, siheks occurred island-wide in all habitats, except pure savannah and wetlands, favoring woodlands and limestone forest areas for feeding and nesting. They lived in diverse habitats, including limestone forests, coastal lowlands, coconut plantations, and even large woody gardens.

Fun Fact #1: Siheks nest in tree cavities, and both sexes participate in nest selection. This seems to play an important role in their pair bonding. The male and female dig out a hole in a decaying tree 10 to 26 feet (3 to 8 meters) above the ground.

Fun Fact #2: The incubation period is 21 to 23 days. Chicks are fed by regurgitation in early stages, with small food items offered thereafter. Fledging is estimated to occur at 33 days.

Fun Fact #3: Siheks hatch with their eyes closed and without any feathers. Because they cannot thermoregulate on their own, the chicks will stay in the nest until they have grown feathers. Their plumage will start to come in at around ten days old, but it will take several more months for the chicks to develop the vibrant blue, orange, and white plumage of adults.

ASIAN WATER DRAGON

Physignathus cocincinus

Where are they from?

Asian water dragons are found in Thailand, Vietnam, Cambodia, Laos, Myanmar (Burma), and southern China. They generally live around permanent standing water, such as on banks of rivers, in rainforests, and in swamps. Water dragons live in areas with an average humidity level ranging from 80 percent in the morning to 60 percent in the evening, and average temperatures of 75 to 85 degrees Fahrenheit (23.8 to 29.4 degrees Celsius).

Fun Fact #1: Females lay between 6 and 15 eggs that hatch after an incubation period of 60 to 75 days.

Fun Fact #2: Hatchlings are about 1 inch (2.54 centimeters) from snout to vent and 5 to 6 inches (13 to 15 centimeters) in total length.

Fun Fact #3: They are often a brown-green color with a pale-green-to-white underside. Light stripes run vertically across each side of their bodies. They also have brown and green banded tails, large eyes, and short snouts.

Fun Fact #4: Life finds a way. Female Asian water dragons can reproduce sexually or asexually—with or without a male. This is called facultative parthenogenesis, and it comes in handy when an animal is trying to repopulate an area and cannot find a mate. While biologists have documented cases of parthenogenesis in other species of squamate reptiles (snakes and lizards), the Smithsonian's National Zoo's Asian water dragon hatchling is the first-known case of parthenogenesis in this species.

GOLDEN-HEADED LION TAMARIN

Leontopithecus chrysomelas

Where are they from?

Golden-headed lion tamarins are found only in Brazil and are endangered. Due to habitat destruction, they are confined to the southern part of the state of Bahia, Brazil. They live in the tall evergreen broadleaf tropical forests and semi-deciduous forests along the Atlantic coast at 10 to 33 feet (3 to 10 meters) in the canopy.

Fun Fact #1: Golden-headed lion tamarins live in family groups of five to seven animals. A typical family group consists of a mated pair plus their youngest offspring. In tamarin society, males and females mate for life and take equal part in raising their young.

Fun Fact #2: Their gestation period lasts about four months. Golden-headed lion tamarins generally reproduce only once a year in the wild.

Fun Fact #3: All family members take part in raising the babies. As the young grow, they learn how to be tamarins from their parents and older siblings. Depending on the size of the family group, the eldest siblings will learn how to carry the babies. Eventually, they start to share that responsibility with the dad. It's great preparation for parenthood in the future!

LOGGERHEAD SHRIKE

Lanius ludovicianus

Where are they from?

Loggerhead shrikes live throughout North America and inhabit open country with short vegetation and well-spaced shrubs or low trees, particularly those with spines or thorns. They frequent agricultural fields, pastures, old orchards, riparian areas, desert scrublands, savannas, prairies, golf courses, and cemeteries. Loggerhead shrikes are often seen along mowed roadsides with access to fence lines and utility poles. Suitable nest trees and perches from which to locate prey are essential components of this species' breeding habitat.

Fun Fact #1: Both sexes help build the nest, which is a solidly constructed but bulky cup of twigs, grass, weeds, and strips of bark lined with softer materials, such as rootlets, animal hair, and feathers. The parents-to-be spend one to two weeks perfecting their nest. The female does most of the work, but the male likes to show her that he is making an effort by bringing the occasional twig or tuft of fur over to her. Most of the time, the female will immediately remove his efforts and continue to make the nest to her liking! She does, however, accept gifts of food from him throughout the process.

Fun Fact #2: Once the nest is "perfect," the female lays her clutch of eggs—one per day—over five or six days. The female is primarily responsible for incubation, which usually lasts 16 to 18 days. During the incubation period, the male supplies the female with food and aggressively defends the nesting territory.

Fun Fact #3: Both adults feed the nestlings. Loggerhead shrike chicks go from hatching to fledging in just over two weeks. As they grow, the fledglings become more mobile and very demanding. The parents have their work cut out for them—bringing food constantly to all their chicks. Chicks stay with their parents for at least three weeks after they fledge.

FENNEC FOX

Vulpes zerda

Where are they from?

Fennec foxes live in North Africa, throughout the Sahara Desert, and also farther east, in the Sinai and Arabia peninsulas. They prefer sandy deserts and arid regions with desert grasses or scrub vegetation.

Fun Fact #1: Fennec foxes typically give birth to one litter of pups per year, with between two and five young in a litter.

Fun Fact #2: Young are born fully furred but blind. Their eyes open after 8 to 11 days, and they are able to walk at about two weeks of age. Pups usually nurse for their first ten weeks of life.

Fun Fact #3: Males defend females before and during birth, and will provide food to the female until the pups are about four weeks old.

Fun fact #4: Pups usually become mature at 9 to 11 months.

ATLANTIC HORSESHOE CRAB

Limulus polyphemus

Where are they from?

The horseshoe crab species found around the United States lives in the Atlantic Ocean along the North American coastline. Atlantic horseshoe crabs are found from Florida to Northern Maine and in the Yucatán peninsula. The largest populations live in the Delaware Bay. There are three other species of horseshoe crab worldwide, located in the Indian Ocean and in two locations in the Pacific Ocean.

Fun Fact #1: From May to early June, horseshoe crabs swarm the beaches to breed and lay eggs. They arrive in huge numbers during high tides that coincide with the full moon or new moon. Females dig nests in the sand and bury a cluster of about 4,000 tiny, blue-green eggs. They can lay about 20 egg clusters each year!

Fun Fact #2: It takes two to four weeks for horseshoe crab eggs to hatch. Tiny crabs emerge, smaller than the eraser on a No. 2 pencil and with nearly see-through shells. The baby horseshoe crabs find shallow, sheltered waters to live in. They molt several times in their first year, shedding their old shells to reveal new shells underneath. Their shells darken as they age. The crabs continue to molt, but with less frequency, as they grow older.

Fun Fact #3: Thousands of shorebirds descend on the Delaware Bay in May to feast on horseshoe crab eggs. Red knots, ruddy turnstones, sanderlings, and other species rely on the protein-packed eggs to power their long flights.

EYELASH PALM PITVIPER

Bothriechis schlegelii

Where are they from?

Eyelash palm pitvipers range from southern Mexico through Central America to Colombia, Ecuador, and western Venezuela, though they have inadvertently been sent throughout the world in banana shipments. Their habitat ranges from densely wooded, sea-level forests, to streamside vegetation in moist lowlands and foothills to wooded cloud and montane forests. They primarily inhabit shrubbery, vine tangles, and low branches of trees and palms.

Fun Fact #1: Eyelash vipers are ovoviviparous. The female snake retains the fertilized eggs inside her body, where each developing baby snake is contained within a fibrous membrane "shell" and nourished by its yolk.

Fun Fact #2: When the baby snakes are fully developed, they either hatch out of the egg membrane inside the oviduct or they hatch just after the membranous eggs are laid by the mother.

Fun Fact #3: Typically, a clutch of eyelash palm pitvipers contains 6 to 12 young, although cases of a clutch with more than 25 have been reported. Newborns are about 6 to 7 inches (15 to 18 centimeters) long.

GREEN ARACARI

Pteroglossus viridis

Where are they from?

Green aracaris inhabit tropical forests in northeast South America, specifically Brazil, French Guiana, Guyana, Suriname, and Venezuela.

Fun Fact #1: Rather than excavating its own hole to build a nest, the green aracari will take over an abandoned woodpecker hole. These existing nesting spots are usually high up in trees.

Fun Fact #2: The female will lay two to four eggs and incubate them for 16 to 19 days.

Fun Fact #3: Chicks fledge about five weeks after hatching. The parents, however, will continue to feed the chicks until they are around six to eight weeks old.

HELLBENDER

Cryptobranchus alleganiensis

Where are they from?

The eastern hellbender's North American range extends from southwestern and south-central New York, west to southern Illinois, and south to extreme northeastern Mississippi and the northern parts of Alabama and Georgia. A separate population occurs in east-central Missouri. A subspecies, the Ozark hellbender (*Cryptobranchus a. bishopii*), exists as an isolated population in southeastern Missouri and adjacent Arkansas. In New York, the hellbender is found solely in the Susquehanna and Allegheny River drainages, including their associated tributaries.

Hellbenders require swift-running, well-oxygenated, unpolluted streams and rivers. An important physical characteristic of these habitats is the presence of riffle areas and abundant large, flat rocks, logs, or boards, which are used for cover and nesting sites.

Fun Fact #1: Males excavate a large nest chamber beneath a rock in preparation for breeding. Pregnant females are either attracted to or corralled into the nest sites by the males.

Fun Fact #2: Females deposit two long strings of 200 to 400 eggs in a softball-sized, yellowish mass onto the nest bed. Males fertilize the eggs externally as the female deposits them. Males then drive out the females and stay in the nest cavity to brood and safeguard the eggs until they hatch 68 to 75 days later.

Fun Fact #3: At hatching, the larvae are about 1 to 1.25 inches (25 to 30 millimeters) in length.

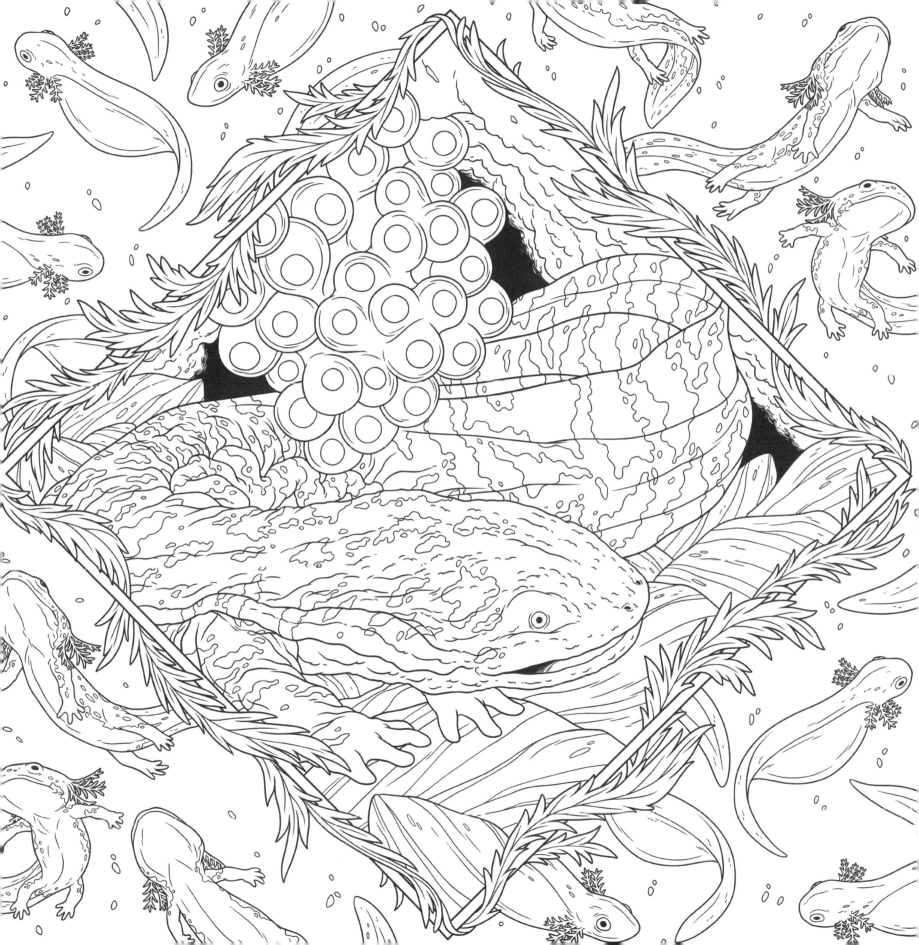

PREHENSILE-TAILED PORCUPINE

Coendou prehensilis

Where are they from?

Prehensile-tailed porcupines live in the South American forests of Venezuela, French Guiana, Brazil, Bolivia, Paraguay, Trinidad, and some extreme northern sections of Argentina. As arboreal animals, they are excellent climbers and spend the majority of their time in trees.

Fun Fact #1: The gestation period lasts about 203 days, resulting in the birth of a single well-developed young that usually weighs about 14 ounces (400 grams).

Fun Fact #2: Prehensile-tailed porcupines are born with their eyes open and are able to climb. Weaning occurs at around ten weeks of age, though the animal does not reach full size until closer to 48 weeks.

Fun Fact #3: At birth, porcupettes have black-and-white quills—they are just very small. The striking rust-colored hair they are born with is also quite sharp and helps them blend in with their environment. Similar to how a person's fingernails get soft after a long swim, the quills are very soft and do not harm the mother at birth, but they do harden within minutes of being exposed to the air. Until the black-and-white quills grow larger and are able to provide a defense mechanism, the porcupette's long, reddish-brown hair provides great camouflage in the tree canopy.

HARTMANN'S MOUNTAIN ZEBRA

Equus zebra

Where are they from?

Hartmann's mountain zebras are a subspecies of the mountain zebra, which is one of three zebra species. Considered vulnerable by the International Union for Conservation of Nature, Hartmann's mountain zebras live in dry mountain habitats in Namibia. Unlike other zebra species, Hartmann's mountain zebras live in small herds, have vertical stripes on their neck and torso, as well as horizontal stripes on their backside, and have a small fold of skin under their chin (called a dewlap). With fewer than 25,000 individuals left in the wild, the biggest threat to this species' survival is habitat loss and fragmentation as the result of livestock production and agriculture.

Fun Fact #1: A zebra's back teeth erupt about two weeks after they are born. Those teeth are especially important for grinding and help the zebra take that big step from nursing to sampling more "adult" foods.

Fun Fact #2: Hartmann's mountain zebra gestation is about one year.

Fun Fact #3: Hartmann's mountain zebras spend most of their time grazing. Even though foals primarily consume milk, around one month old they show interest in eating grass, plucking blades, tossing them about, and playing with them.

LINNAEUS'S TWO-TOED SLOTH

Choloepus didactylus

Where are they from?

Sloths are found throughout Central America and northern South America, including parts of Brazil and Peru. They live high in the trees of tropical rainforests, where they spend most of their time curled up or hanging upside down from branches.

Fun Fact #1: Sloths will sleep, eat, mate, and even give birth upside down!

Fun Fact #2: After a gestation period of six months, they give birth to small, well-developed babies that measure approximately 10 inches (25 centimeters) long and weigh about 12 ounces (340 grams).

Fun Fact #3: Baby sloths cling to their mother's belly for five weeks, until they are strong enough to move on their own. Mothers spend a lot of time and energy feeding and caring for them, both before and after the young are weaned.

CHEETAH

Acinonyx jubatus

Where are they from?

Cheetahs inhabit a broad section of Africa, including areas of North Africa, the Sahel, and eastern and southern Africa. Over the past 50 years, cheetahs have become extinct in at least 13 countries, and they are currently most prevalent in Kenya and Tanzania in East Africa, and Namibia and Botswana in southern Africa. The Asiatic cheetah is known to survive in Iran but is critically endangered. Cheetahs thrive in areas with vast expanses of land where prey is abundant.

Fun Fact #1: A cheetah's gestation period is about three months, and the average litter size is three to six cubs.

Fun Fact #2: Cubs are smoky gray in color, with long hair called a mantle running along their backs. On average, they are about 12 inches (30 centimeters) long and weigh 9 to 12 ounces (255 to 340 grams) at birth.

Fun Fact #3: When they are about six months old, the mother will capture live prey for them to practice killing.

DAMA GAZELLE

Nanger dama

Where are they from?

The dama gazelle's historical range included the desert and arid zones of Chad (eastern), and the Darfur and Kordofan Provinces of Sudan. Due to wars in their range, habitat destruction, desertification, overhunting, and human and livestock population expansion, they are now extremely rare, occurring only as vagrants or in pockets. Dama gazelles are critically endangered, which means they face a very high risk of extinction in the wild. The wild population has dropped precipitously in the past 20 years, with a scant 400 estimated to remain in the wild.

Fun Fact #1: Much of what is known about reproduction comes from animal husbandry experience in human care. The gestation is approximately six and a half months, resulting in a single offspring. Twinning is very rare.

Fun Fact #2: Reproductive scientists at the Zoo are conducting fecal hormone studies on dama gazelles at both the Zoo and the Smithsonian's Conservation Biology Institute. They are working to gather baseline hormone data to determine onset of puberty and breeding patterns in both sexes, estrus cycle in females, and gestation timing and duration.

Fun Fact #3: Dama gazelles make an endearing "honk" noise when alerted to danger! Gazelles will suck air in through their noses until they have a crinkled or deflated look. When they release the air, the vocalization sounds like a honk. Each individual's sounds different, and the tone varies in length and pitch. Calves learn this behavior from a young age. They crinkle their noses and try to honk, but they barely make any noise.

FRESHWATER STINGRAY

Potamotrygon castexi, Potamotrygon leopoldi, Potamotrygon motoro

Where are they from?

Freshwater stingrays are native to South America and Asia. As their name implies, they live in fresh water in the Amazon and the Mekong River. This is in contrast to most cartilaginous fish, which live in a saltwater environment.

Fun Fact #1: The unborn young are ovoviviparous, meaning they are nourished by egg yolk inside the mother's body. After a gestation period of three months, the female produces eggs that hatch internally before birth. The developing embryos receive additional nutrition from a rich milky substance produced in the mother's uterus.

Fun Fact #2: About one litter of two to six pups is produced yearly. When a ray is born, its disc is about 3 inches (8 centimeters) wide.

MELLER'S CHAMELEON

Trioceros melleri

Where are they from?

Meller's chameleons inhabit treetops within savanna, woodland, and mountain regions of Malawi, Mozambique, and Tanzania. They are the largest chameleons on the mainland of Africa. Adults can grow to be two feet (61 centimeters) long and weigh over one pound (453 grams).

Fun Fact #1: After copulation, females can store sperm for several months and lay several clutches after breeding just one time. Females deposit their eggs into a hole in the ground, burying the eggs with leaves.

Fun Fact #2: The common name of the Meller's chameleon is the "giant one-horned chameleon." That's because males and females both sport a horn at the end of their nose. Scientists have not determined what the function of the horn is, if it has any function at all. Many lizards have crests and other adornments that don't serve an obvious purpose, but there are some theories that these horns can be used as a means of defense or during combat.

Fun Fact #3: Chameleons are well known for their ability to change colors. But they don't do that to camouflage themselves. Instead, they change color based upon their mood. Typically, their skin has a banded yellow-and-green pattern. If a male is trying to woo a female, however, he might put on a fantastic display of color—vibrant blues, greens, and yellows that pop. If the female is receptive, she will respond with bright colors as well. If they are not receptive, or if they become angry or stressed, their skin will darken, and black spots will appear.

WHITE-NAPED CRANE

Grus vipio

Where are they from?

White-naped cranes are native to northern Mongolia, southern Siberia, Korea, Japan, and central China. They are found in grassy marshes, wet sedge meadows and reedbeds in broad river valleys, lake depressions, and boggy upland wetlands. They prefer areas where their nests can be concealed and there is little grazing pressure.

Fun Fact #1: Mated pairs of cranes, including white-naped cranes, engage in unison calling, which is a complex and extended series of coordinated calls. Female white-naped cranes initiate the display and utter two calls for each male call.

Fun Fact #2: Nests are mounds of dried sedges and grasses in open wetlands. Females usually lay two eggs, two or three days apart, and incubation (by both sexes) lasts 28 to 32 days. Both parent birds take part in building the nest, incubating the eggs, and rearing the chicks.

Fun Fact #3: White-naped crane chicks have yellow-brown feathers and pink-gray bills, legs, and feet. They are fed by both parents and fledge about 70 to 75 days after hatching.

Fun Fact #4: All cranes engage in dancing, which includes various behaviors such as bowing, jumping, running, stick or grass tossing, and wing flapping. Dancing can occur at any age and is commonly associated with courtship. It is, however, generally believed to be a normal part of motor development for cranes and can serve to thwart aggression, relieve tension, and strengthen pair bonds.

SOUTHERN TAMANDUA

Tamandua tetradactyla

Where are they from?

Tamanduas are found throughout much of South America: throughout all of Guyana, Trinidad and Tobago, Suriname, French Guiana, Brazil, and Paraguay. This species also inhabits parts of Uruguay, Argentina, Bolivia, Peru, Ecuador, Colombia, and Venezuela. An adaptable species, southern tamanduas can be found in forests, savannas, tropical rainforests, scrub forests, and mangroves, but they most commonly live near streams and rivers. They have been documented at elevations reaching 6,500 feet (2,000 meters).

Fun Fact #1: Pregnancy lasts between 130 and 150 days, after which a single offspring is born. Twin births can occur but are uncommon.

Fun Fact #2: As with other species of anteaters, mothers carry young tamanduas on their backs throughout the first months of life. Young remain with their mother for about one year before reaching sexual maturity and heading off on their own.

Fun Fact #3: Tamanduas primarily consume ants and termites, and in the wild they can eat as many as 9,000 insects a day! With such a specialized diet, tamanduas have some unique adaptations for eating. Since their mouth only opens to about the width of a pencil eraser, they have a sticky 16-inch-long tongue that allows them to navigate ant and termite nests and quickly consume their prey.

SPIDER TORTOISE

Pyxis arachnoides

Where are they from?

Spider tortoises are found only in a narrow belt of dry forest along the southwestern coast of Madagascar. This species faces an uncertain future in its native habitat, Madagascar's unique Spiny Forest. The Spiny Forest is a harsh ecosystem that takes highly specialized species to survive in it. The ecological changes and alterations to this ecosystem by humans is causing a steady population decline. In addition, the small size of these tortoises and their beautiful shell patterns make them popular to illegally collect for the pet trade and food markets around the world. You can help these tortoises, too, by refraining from purchasing animals or animal products that were taken out of Madagascar.

Fun Fact #1: Female spider tortoises only lay one egg per clutch, so populations cannot quickly recover from a decrease in numbers.

Fun Fact #2: The tortoise eggs incubate for about 220 to 250 days before hatching.

Fun Fact #3: When spider tortoises hatch, they're on their own. Neither parent provides for their young.

Fun Fact #4: Spider tortoises show no sexual dimorphism when they are young. It may take 12 to 15 years before animal keepers can confirm if a hatchling is male or female.

LEMUR LEAF FROG

Agalychnis lemur

Where are they from?

Lemur frogs are native to the humid tropical forests of Central America, namely Panama and Costa Rica. They live in forests on sloping mountainsides and in the humid uplands and lowlands. The rainy season begins in March and can last for several months. When the rain is at its heaviest, it triggers the frogs' breeding season. These frogs have been extirpated, or wiped out, of parts of their previous range and are critically endangered where they currently live.

Fun Fact #1: Lemur frogs reach adulthood between one and a half to two years. Fully grown, the males are only about half the size of the females. Males also have a modified digit on each front foot—called a "nuptial pad"—which helps them clasp onto the females when breeding.

Fun Fact #2: Male frogs begin their courtship by singing or calling to attract females. If a female is receptive and approaches, he may try to grasp onto her from behind. This position is called "amplexus." As the female lays her eggs, the male fertilizes them externally. Once the male has completed this task, he moves on to "woo" the next female. Although the female might stay on the leaf for a day or two, she leaves the eggs on their own soon after.

Fun Fact #3: Females will only deposit their eggs on leaves or branches located over water. The ideal spot seems to be a smooth, hidden surface, like the underside of a leaf.

Fun Fact #4: Once the embryos develop, they wiggle and push out of their jelly-like egg and fall off the leaf, down into the water below. The tadpoles will complete the rest of their developmental life stage—referred to as "metamorphosis"—over the next 40 to 60 days. Once the final stages of metamorphosis are finished, the frogs come out of the water as miniature versions of the adults. At that stage, they are called "froglets."

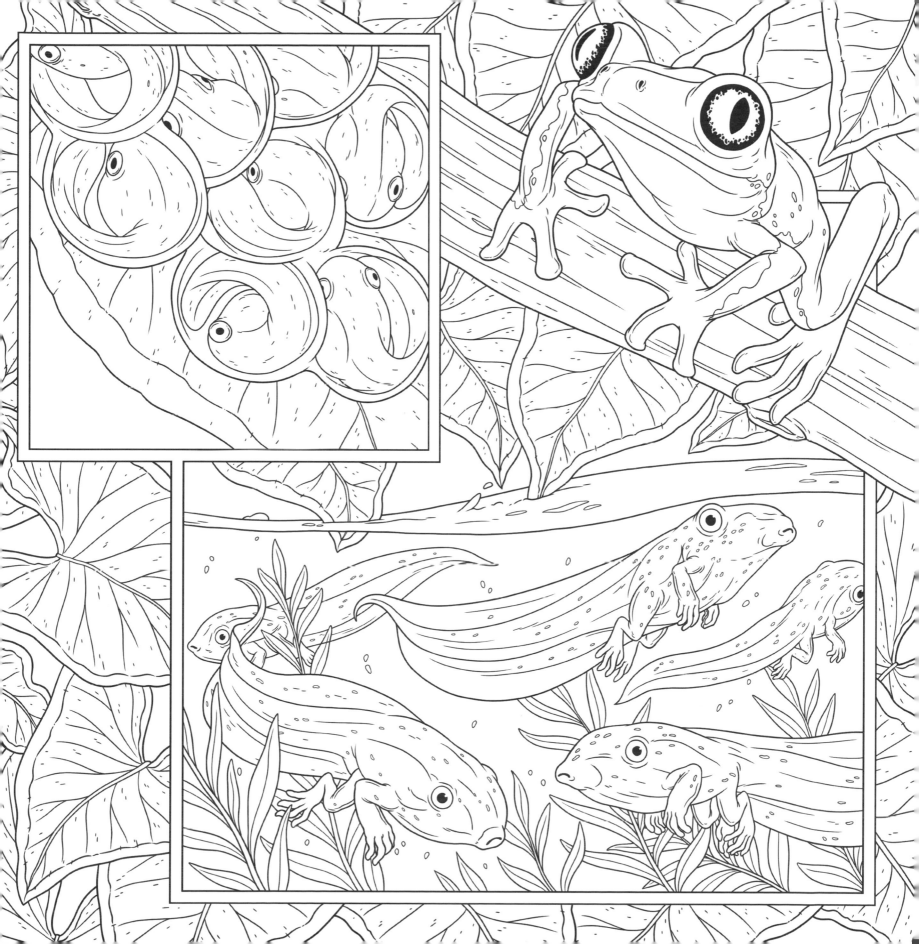

CALIFORNIA SEA LION

Zalophus californianus

Where are they from?

The three species of California sea lion are divided by geographical divisions—in the eastern North Pacific, from British Columbia to Baja California; in the Gulf of California; and in a separate population on the Galapagos Islands. California sea lions are not typically found more than 10 miles (16 kilometers) from the Pacific coastline. They usually congregate on islands and remote shorelines when not in the ocean.

Fun Fact #1: Females give birth to a single pup and are protective of them for several days, moving the pups around with them. Females then begin to leave their pups for increasing lengths of time.

Fun Fact #2: Pups are about 2.5 feet (75 centimeters) long, nose to tail tip, and weigh about 18 pounds (8 kilograms) at birth. They are chestnut brown in color.

Fun Fact #3: Young pups nurse at frequent intervals throughout the day, but by three weeks old are left alone for increasing amounts of time. Pups gather in groups, called colonies, and spend their time resting, exploring the rookery, and playing in tide pools. They nurse anywhere from six months to a year, until the arrival of the next pup.

WESTERN LOWLAND GORILLA

Gorilla gorilla gorilla

Where are they from?

Western lowland gorillas are broadly distributed across the Congo Basin and are continuously distributed across the countries of Gabon, Central Africa Republic, Cameroon, Angola, Equatorial Guinea, and Congo. Though present historically in the Democratic Republic of Congo, they are now likely extinct there. They are a critically endangered species that has been plagued by exceptionally high levels of disease and hunting, which has resulted in a population decline of over sixty percent in the past 20 to 25 years.

Fun Fact #1: There is no set time of year for gorilla births. Western lowland gorilla gestation lasts about eight and a half months. Birth typically occurs in a supine position over the course of a few minutes to several hours. The offspring are not born helpless. They have an instinctive grasp behavior seen in other primates that allows them to hold on to their mothers' chests.

Fun Fact #2: Mothers can be seen supporting the infants for the first few months of life. Birth weight averages 4 pounds (2 kilograms). For the first couple of years, gorilla infants grow at twice the rate of a human baby. They can crawl and ride on their mothers' backs at three months old. They may continue to ride on their mothers' backs, chests, or legs until they are three and a half to four years old.

Fun Fact #3: A small white tuft of hair on the infants' rumps distinguishes them up to four years old. The white patch helps the mother keep track of the infant and assists other group members in identifying the gorilla as an infant.

BAND-TAILED PIGEON

Patagioenas fasciata

Where are they from?

Band-tailed pigeons live in mature coniferous forests across North American western mountains, damp forests of the West Coast, and conifer-oak woodlands, into Mexico, Central, and South America. They also visit forested suburban parks, fields, and orchards.

Fun Fact #1: Males and females take turns incubating the eggs for 16 to 22 days.

Fun Fact #2: Even though adult band-tailed pigeons are a blue-gray hue, their chicks are yellow and fuzzy.

EUROPEAN GLASS LIZARD

Pseudopus apodus

Where are they from?

Their range is large—throughout eastern Europe and parts of Asia—but the rocky outcroppings where they live are being bulldozed for construction and development projects.

Fun Fact #1: Glass lizard eggs are about the size of a ping-pong ball, but their shape is more oval than round.

Fun Fact #2: Once glass lizard offspring emerge from their shells, they are on their own. Both hatchlings and adults use their keen eyesight to detect any motion from potential prey.

Fun Fact #3: Glass lizards get their name from their tail, which breaks and shatters very easily—just like glass—as a defense mechanism.

Fun Fact #4: Glass lizards are solitary in the wild, but they can be found together during breeding season. Because they don't have arms, legs, or hands, a male holds on to a female by placing his mouth on her neck and biting down. Potentially, he could injure her in doing so, but, for the most part, the marks he leaves are superficial. Once she sheds her skin, they are all gone.

Smithsonian

Baby ANIMALS

Coloring Book